Bereft and Blessed

ALSO BY JOAN SELIGER SIDNEY

Body of Diminishing Motion (CavanKerry Press)

The Way the Past Comes Back (The Kutenai Press)

Bereft and Blessed

Poems by

Joan Seliger Sidney

Antrim House
Simsbury, Connecticut

Copyright © 2014 by Joan Seliger Sidney

Except for short selections appearing in book reviews,
all reproduction rights are reserved. Requests
for permission to reprint should be
sent to the publisher.

Library of Congress Control Number: 2014933628

ISBN: 978-1-936482-64-1

Printed & bound by United Graphics, Inc.

Cover art by Gray Jacobik:
detail from "The Stunned Amethystine Sea"
encaustic, 10" x 10" x 2"
(the full work in black & white on p. iii)

Author Photograph by Suzy Staubach

Antrim House
860.217.0023
AntrimHouse@comcast.net
www.AntrimHouseBooks.com
21 Goodrich Road, Simsbury, CT 06070

For Stu, again and always

For our children and granddaughters: Dan and Naomi, Ray, Larry, Jen and Marco; Josephine, Amelia, Tali, Ruby, and Shari

For my best brother, Ralph

and in memory of Joan Joffe Hall, first poetry mentor, beloved friend

and also in memory of my very dear cousins, Ruth and Sharoni

ACKNOWLEDGMENTS

These poems first appeared, sometimes in earlier versions, or are forthcoming in the following publications, to whose editors grateful acknowledgment is made:

Alimentum: "Our Table"; *Caduceus:* "A Bielski Partisan Speaks," "Cousin," "Hiding from the Nazis," "My Cousin Tells How His Brother Found Him," "Pantoum for My Grandparents," "Rue Ordener, Rue Labat," "Why My Mother Can't Speak Yiddish"; *Jewish Currents:* "Cousin," "Hills and Valleys," "Latkes"; *Long River Review:* "Two-Headed Horses"; *Momentum:* "Regrets"; *The Louisville Review:* "First MS Attack"; *Theodate:* "Hello, Good-Bye"; *Touching MS: Poetic Expressions:* "Multiple Sclerosis"; *24 Pearl: The Magazine:* "I Wake with Tears"; *Zurawno website:* "Zurawno Ladies' Auxiliary."

I would like to thank the Connecticut Commission on Culture and Tourism for an Individual Artist Fellowship and the Connecticut Office of the Arts for including "My Cousin Tells How His Brother Found Him" and "Pantoum for My Grandparents" in "Now & Then: An Exhibition of Artist Fellowship Recipients"; and the Craig H. Nielsen Foundation for their fellowship to the Vermont Studio Center (the greatest artists' colony, where I worked on the first draft of this book) which even paid for my personal care assistant (thanks, Ryan Walsh, Tandy Belt, Crescent Dragonwagon!).

I am grateful to Sharon Bryan, Darcie Dennigan, Carolyn Forché, Lisa Rowe Fraustino, Margaret Gibson, Lesléa Newman, Betsy Sholl, and most especially to Robert Cording and Penelope Pelizzon for their insightful comments and generosity; to Rennie McQuilkin, my dedicated editor and publisher; to Arnold Dashefsky, Jeffrey Shoulson, Lorri Lafontaine, Rae Asselin, and the Center for Judaic Studies and Contemporary Jewish Life; to my family for much love and inspiration, and especially to Stu, who has journeyed with me through every draft of every poem, and to my late mother, who remains my Muse.

TABLE OF CONTENTS

The Self / 2

I. INHERITANCE

Why My Mother Can't Speak Yiddish / 4
Inheritance / 6
Our Table / 7
I Wake with Tears / 9
Hiding from the Nazis / 10
A Bielski Partisan Speaks / 12
Pantoum for My Grandparents / 14
My Mother Writes a Letter Home / 15
Rue Ordener, Rue Labat / 17
Cousin / 19
My Cousin Tells How His Brother Found Him / 20
Fleeing / 21
Photographer and Coachman / 22
Edward Finds a Photograph from Zurawno, 1942 / 23
On Approaching Seventy / 24

II. HILLS AND VALLEYS

Photo of Avenue J Park / 26
Photo: Two-headed Horses / 27
Hello, Goodbye / 28
Zurawno Ladies' Auxiliary / 31
Dream: the Hanging / 32
Dialogue / 34
First MS Attack / 35
Regrets / 36
Multiple Sclerosis / 38
Like Sisters, an Elegy / 41

Trails / 44
Latkes / 45
Ribbons / 46
The Cough / 51
Rescue / 53
Voices / 55
First Visit to Maggie's Ranch / 57
Hills and Valleys / 58
Sharoni, Remember / 60
For My Friend Fighting Breast Cancer / 61
Kathy Shaughnessy Jambeck / 62
For Better or Worse / 63
There's No App for That / 64
Possibilities / 65
In My Dream / 66
Le Chemin de Guérison Intérieure: Road of Inner Healing / 67

NOTES / 70

ABOUT THE AUTHOR / 73

ABOUT THE BOOK / 74

All journeys have secret destinations of which the traveler is unaware.

— Martin Buber

Bereft and Blessed

THE SELF

It is small and likes to disappear
in a thicket of blackberry brambles,

making it tricky to pursue. It runs
quickly, skimming sky.

It never sits still. It picks
a peach in passing or snags an apple.

It breathes beetles and butterflies
instead of air.

I. Inheritance

WHY MY MOTHER
CAN'T SPEAK YIDDISH

"I know," Mom tells me, "when they were alone
Papa and Mama spoke Yiddish
like the other old Zurawno
Jews. But although I know a few
words like Papa's *Du host genug gekvetsht!*

whenever one of us seven children
complained too much, in our home we spoke
Polish." *Not to have a Yiddish
accent,* Mama said. "When I asked,
what's an accent and why was it bad,

she looked me hard in the eyes
and took both my hands. I felt chills
and squeezed tight, wishing
I could pull those questions back
into my mouth." "*Christ killers,*"

*the Poles call Jews. But if you speak
real Polish, with no accent,
they won't know and you'll be safe.*
"Mama pulled me tight
against her chest. Barely could I breathe

but who cared? At night I listened
to Mama and Papa's Yiddish
whispers slip through our wall
like *Rozinkes mit Mandlen*
lullabying me to sleep."

"Some story, Mom! Makes me
want to learn Yiddish."
I take her spotted hands, kiss
her wrinkled cheeks, inhale her scented
breath: baked apples, cinnamon, Sanka.

INHERITANCE

Zurawno, Poland, where Mom grew up:
The coal stove in the kitchen, brick
oven big enough for her mama
to bake wheat bread, challah, rugelach
to feed her family of nine all week.
The chestnut table doubling
as the goose-down feather bed
where Mom and her sister Luba slept.
The barn behind the house, the cow
her sister Minka milked morning and night.
The eggs Mom picked up from the sixteen hens
she gave grain, named, and refused to eat,
not even in Shabbos soup.
The outhouse in the woods
she wouldn't use on icy days and nights.
Her brother Julik's hickory skis
she borrowed, ropes threaded
through holes and tied to her boots;
the Carpathian trails she crisscrossed,
the cheese and chocolate she stopped to eat.
The Dniester, where Srulik, Julik's best friend,
taught her the European breaststroke,
her head high above water.
Her blue eyes that speared him for life.
Their courtship off and on: Gymnasium in Lwow
for her, law studies in Krakow for him.
This pink heart-shaped diamond engagement ring
Dad slipped on Mom's fourth finger,
at home today on mine.

OUR TABLE

Days when
relatives come
to visit and stay for
nights, the kitchen table becomes
our bed.

Luba
and I keep warm
with goosefeather pillows,
quilt. "If not for Mama's shaking
the coal

stove, we'd
sleep till breakfast,"
Luba groans, scowls. Mama
needs to heat the room before we
can eat.

Mama
shovels in coal,
sweeps ashes off the floor,
washes her black hands, peels and grates
potatoes,

onions,
beats eggs, adds matzoh
meal, oil, mixes kugel
then slides the pan into our brick
oven.

It hurts
my eyes to see
Mama work non-stop hard.
I set out plates, cups, napkins, knives,
slice bread

and cheese
by myself while
Princess Luba, Mama
jokes, oversees. With both eyes closed,
I think.

I WAKE WITH TEARS

Sometimes in my dreams I hear
Mom's voice sing the silence
of her orchard, row after row
of branches broken, her house
a ghost lost between wars,
her parents a photo
snapped by a soldier.

   *   *   *

Sometimes in the orchard
of memory, wild horses race
past Mom's house, stolen
by her Ukrainian neighbors
after a stranger led her
through the forest of blue spruce,
no road but pine needles for bed,
no fire but dreams to sing.

   *   *   *

Sometimes in the snow
of sleep I hear Mom's voice
break through like a lost friend
on a ghost road going somewhere
I can't remember — the river
of her words, the moon of her
history, her grief.

HIDING FROM THE NAZIS

I am reading about Yosef Laufer, how
this 17-year-old and his father survived
the Nazi occupation, when a sentence
startles me out of their lives

into mine. *For six months we hide
with the family of Yisroel Reiss.*
Can they be the grandparents
I never knew? I have just one

sepia photo, snapped by a passing
soldier, *Zurawno, 1935* penciled
on the back. My grandparents stare
straight ahead, believing

there will always be cattle
for him to fatten and sell, potatoes
for her to serve, steaming with cream.
I want to know more

about these two, but first Laufer
writes about the empty space
between the toilet and the loft
where, each time an *Aktion* began

they all stood hunched, hiding
from the Germans, Ukrainians,
Judenrat Jews. From the food
scraps left by those Jews

rounded up, from the wheat
and flour bartered, Grandma
cooked for five. *She washed
our clothes and tried to keep*

*the house clean. Noble...
but...pedantic,* Yosef wrote.
Does that mean in the ghetto
world of chaos, Grandma

worked to make order?
Or a word mistranslated
from his penciled notes?
I want to know why

when the five crossed
to the "Aryan" side, heading
for the open fields, the oldest,
my grandparents went first.

"Stop or I'll shoot!" Yosef
heard a Ukrainian cry. No
gunshots, no shouts, silence.
He never saw them again.

A BIELSKI PARTISAN SPEAKS

Victory means each day
we stay human. Steal

only to eat, take from farms
rich in potatoes and turnips;

not from farmers starving
like us, fields stripped, barns

burned, cows, pigs, chickens
slaughtered by Germans. Deep in the forest

in darkness we cook our soup, the black
pot hangs from a branch, fire blazes

below. Safe for a few hours, no Germans
brave enough to enter the night forest.

Still we sleep dressed, ready
to flee our temporary tents

of tree leaves and limbs. What
a strange collection of runaway

Jews, our Bielski *otriad!* Old
people, young men and women,

children. To Tuvia Bielski,
who leads us on his horse

like a meteor, everyone is welcome.
Some younger men disagree, fear

for food, want revenge. "Feel free
to leave," Tuvia tells them. "Better

to save one Jew than to kill twenty
Germans." Not so for Belorusian peasants

who catch fleeing ghetto Jews,
keep them freezing in storage

rooms overnight, tie them up
like sheep, and sell them to the police.

With their own guns, Tuvia shoots them
and their families. On their farm doors,

in Russian he writes: *Death to Nazi
collaborators.* Now they know

we Jews, too, can fight. Our *otriad*
grows to a forest *shtetl,* our own Jerusalem.

July 1944: our exodus stretches almost
two kilometers – scouts on horseback, marching

fighters, horse-drawn carts for the sick,
a herd of cows, a celebration of survivors.

PANTOUM FOR MY GRANDPARENTS

On Yom Kippur I wrote my first Holocaust poem
instead of returning to synagogue to pray.
The grandmother I never knew put her
hands on my shoulders and told me her story.

Instead of returning to synagogue to pray,
back to Zurawno I journeyed with Grandma.
Hands on my shoulders, she told me her story:
"Germans, so cultured, won't hurt us old Jews."

Back to Zurawno I journeyed with Grandma.
We watched the road darken with soldiers.
"Germans, so cultured, won't hurt us old Jews.
From us, our Ukrainian neighbors rent."

We watched the road darken with soldiers.
Grandpa wore his Silver Cross from World War I.
"From us, our Ukrainian neighbors rent."
If, only instead of listening, I'd whisked them away.

Grandpa wore his Silver Cross from World War I.
Grandma braided challah and slid it in the oven.
If, only instead of listening, I'd whisked them away
before the betrayal by their Ukrainian neighbors.

Grandma braided challah and slid it in the oven.
She braised brisket and potatoes, my mouth watered
before the betrayal by her Ukrainian neighbors.
They beat and bloodied Grandma and Grandpa.

She braised brisket and potatoes, my mouth watered.
Granddaughter from the future, what could I do?
Neighbors beat and bloodied Grandma and Grandpa,
threw their still-breathing bodies into a pit for Jews.

MY MOTHER WRITES
A LETTER HOME

New York, July 1941

Three weeks already since I waved
to the green lady and her torch.
We docked in Hoboken. What a crowd
waiting to see relatives walk
down the gangplank! It's like Zurawno
when everyone waited for Prince Czartoryski
and his family to ride by.

A handsome man called to me. American-
born. By his "Hello," I could tell. At his side,
a black briefcase, the smell of fine leather.
I thought of Papa's saddle on its shelf
in our barn and those times when
I wrapped my hands around his waist
as we clopped happily along the Dniester.

Stamped on the man's briefcase,
the mysterious letters HIAS.
"We help Jewish immigrants
find apartments, jobs," he said. But
before I could sign my name,
like the Dybbuk, Luba caught me
with one hand and wouldn't let go.

Her other scrunched his piece of paper,
threw it in the street. "No charity."
Her eyes on fire. "My sister
lives with me."

How can I be ungrateful
after the affidavit she sent? Three years
in Belgrade checking the chalkboard
for my name. The Polish quota two visas
a day. "Do you think I give visas
like chocolate?" the American Consul said.

But, Mama, you should see
where Luba lives. Her family of four
in an apartment smaller than the coop
for our few hens. On the floor I sleep
with no featherbed. A blanket so thin
you could count threads. Black coffee
and crumbs for breakfast. Milk
and eggs for the children only.
When Abie works, he cuts fur. Most days
with their signs, he and others
from the shop walk up and down
the street. WORKERS
STRIKE TO UNIONIZE!

At the newsstand, I read want ads.
After my eight years of Latin,
five of Greek, floors and toilets
should I scrub? No nickel
for the trolley, block after block
after block I walk and knock.

RUE ORDENER, RUE LABAT

Paris, 16 July 1942: Sarah Kofman, you were nine the night the Nazis
knocked for your father, a Polish rabbi. At 60 you still hear your mother:
"He's at his synagogue, praying." You still see him open
their bedroom door. "I am here. Take me." He believed
he could trade his life for his wife and six children. Believed
the Germans were reasonable people. Strangers

helped your mother escape to the countryside.
One by one she gave away your brothers and sisters.
But you refused to eat pork, forcing her to take you.
She tried to hide you at the Jewish Children's Home on rue Lamarque.
Your fingers wouldn't let go. You two remained on

rue Ordener. In your ears the others' voices stole your sleep.
Only one postcard from Drancy, not your father's slant or squiggle.
One night a man you didn't know knocked. "Midnight
the next round-up. Your names are on the list." Your mother
left everything, even the photograph of her dead parents.

The man sent you to rue Labat, still 18th arrondissement,
six blocks south. A blonde in a black nightgown
opened her door "for one night," but let you stay the war.
Suzanne she called you, never Sarah. Unlike your mother,
Mémé hugged and kissed you.
When sirens sent you to the Metro shelter,
she held you so tight her wool sweater scratched your cheeks.
Her hands crushed your ears but still you heard bombs explode,
glass shatter, people scream and die.

At quiet times, Mémé held your hand as you walked
the neighborhood, passing as her daughter.

Once you stopped in your old courtyard. Your dresser
with your butterfly collection in the top drawer, each specimen
pinned to blue paper, lay under bricks and broken glass.
She taught you to eat pork, steak fried in butter,
to cross yourself in church. She filled you with stories
of *When the war ends...*

But after the Liberation of Paris, your mother
tore you from Mémé. When your brothers and sisters returned
from their Catholic homes, like Joseph's brothers they hated you.
Your father had been beaten by a guard and buried alive
at Auschwitz, a skeleton said. Only Mémé encouraged you.
From her pocket, your university texts and fees. At the Sorbonne,
Sarah Kofman, you became professor of philosophy, a feminist
and deconstructionist. "I wasn't able to go to her funeral. But
at her grave the priest said she had saved a little Jewish girl
during the war," you wrote in your memoir, *Rue Ordener,
Rue Labat,* and not long after that, you took your life.

COUSIN

Jan Rybak, the tiniest man
in his village, opens his attic
to a man and his eight-year-old
daughter, her mother killed
while fleeing camp. He shares
his potatoes, ignores the law:
death to any Christian
and his family that helps a Jew.

When Nazi soldiers drag
a teenage girl over cobblestones,
her legs bloody, her dress
shreds, the crowd shrieking
Jude! Jude! Jan Rybak
grabs her hand, hoists her up
into his buggy, her eyes wide
with disbelief. "She's not a Jude!"
he shouts to his townspeople.
"She's my cousin."

MY COUSIN TELLS HOW
HIS BROTHER FOUND HIM

Of Father's other family, I knew nothing
until last spring. An e-mail from Marek
Ostern — my patronymic too —
revealed the secret my parents
took to their graves. I believe him
without seeing the copy of "our" father's
medical diploma he says he possesses.

*If you don't recognize it,
it doesn't exist* was how my parents
lived after the Holocaust. Father's private
practice became a goldmine of the sick.
My mother wore mink, my father
drove a pink Lincoln. Even once
did Father send money
to Marek and his mother?

All those years an only child,
how I longed for a brother. Like me,
Marek has blue eyes
and red hair that's turned gray.

FLEEING

God knows where they're going
      in this photo by Josef Koudelka,
           this stream of refugees caught by camera

almost in a pose. Up front, the family
      dog, white chest and forelegs, regal
           and high as a Weimaraner, pulls

the two-wheeled cart, his withers yoked.
      The child, awkwardly balanced on a bundle
           of clothes, struggles to stay seated.

Like sticks beating his back, sacks
      stuffed with pans, pots, potatoes, barley —
           everything and nothing his parents could fit

in this quick exodus — shift and hit.
      Alongside, his mother in her everyday
           dress and shawl, his father in his peaked

wool cap stare straight ahead, not daring
      to blink at the camera, trying not to see
           black boots, Kalashnikovs blocking the border.

PHOTOGRAPHER AND COACHMAN

Roman Vishniac *had* to visit his father's
birthplace. Slonim, 1937: Poland,
Belarus before and after. His train late, night
a rainy chill. At the end of the square

a coachman in woolens transparently thin
drove him to an inn. "Pay me when you leave,
not tonight." Photo after photo
Vishniac snapped: the Great Synagogue,

Yeshiva, school for boys, hospital, orphanage,
three sisters on the bridge over the Szczara
River, Jewish street vendors, families huddled
together in one or two rooms, food shelves bare.

Days later, back to the station. "Your fee
for two trips?" Vishniac asked. "Two trips
only? Who will pay the freezing nights
I waited? My home an empty cupboard. My infant

son in a tiny coffin, buried by borrowed money."
Vishniac embraced the coachman, turned
his pockets inside out. Each *zloty*
heated the man's hands. The photographer
ran, jumped up to catch the moving train.

EDWARD FINDS A PHOTOGRAPH FROM ZURAWNO, 1942

Who snapped this black and white
of Frederik, my older brother
and his friends? Except
for Igor, who's Gentile, everyone's

wearing armbands. Look at Henya,
my dreamsecret. Like Hedy Lamarr,
black hair tucked back. Mama used to say,
"After we're saved, she'll marry

an American officer." For a few months
before the *Aktion,* all of us
squeezed together in one room, a world
away from the house we used to rent

from Henya's parents in the building
they owned before. Behind her, Ezio,
Papa's partner's son. Eyes like coal,
body thin as a fox. Nights

we raided neighbor's fields
for potatoes to take home. Never,
never enough. Papa lay in bed,
heels swollen from starvation.

ON APPROACHING SEVENTY

Watching the hands of my son
kneading challah dough
on the maple cutting board
in my kitchen, a memory

rises of my mother
bending over our kitchen table
in Flatbush, pressing, stretching,
folding flour, water, eggs

into a living elastic.
Sometimes in my dreams, Mom
appears, whispers of her mother
in her kitchen in Zurawno

in the pre-dawn dark,
by the light of the kerosene
lamp, pulling and pushing
the yeasty challah dough

until my son covers it
with a clean white cloth
and leaves it in the warm
electric oven to rise.

II. Hills and Valleys

PHOTO OF AVENUE J PARK

I know that road, those pebbles that sneak between my toes.
I know that bench, thick wood slats bolted to concrete.

That bump-me-up-and-down seesaw. Those monkey
bars I scoot across hand-over-hand. The stroller

parked nearby, that bratty boy sucking a zwieback.
I know that mama, her open coat catching spring breezes,

her hair a bird's nest bobby-pinned on top of her head.
She sees me dig in the dirt, pile pebbles in a heap.

She tells me to pick handfuls of chamomile flowers, weaves
a wreath to crown my curls. From her pocket, she pulls a hanky.

With her spit, she cleans my fingers. Peels an apple for me.
She unscrews a thermos, pours me a cup of milk.

My head sinks heavy in her lap, she lullabies me to sleep.
Rozynkies mit mandlen, song from somewhere disappeared.

PHOTO: TWO-HEADED HORSES

What's left of summer? Two two-headed horses
at sunset. Where's the rest of their carousel?

Nickel a ride, grab the gold ring, next course's
free. Where are the kids who rode till night fell?

How long ago was I the child who ran
across the trolley tracks at Coney Island,

who jumped the waves and built castles in sand?
No dunes to climb, Bay Nine, flat as my hand.

On nights when Dad worked late, we ate Nathan's
hot dogs, salty French fries, strolled the Boardwalk.

Dizzy from sun, sea and fireworks, we heathens
forgot our fourth-floor walk-up. Mom talked

about swimming the Dniester, on the banks of her town;
how Dad rescued a man who would've drowned.

HELLO, GOOD-BYE

As a child in Flatbush, *shalom*
meant hello. "Hello, Mr. Soniker,"
who Tuesdays after school taught me
to read Hebrew. I still hear him

scraping his throat. Six of us hid —
five boys and I — behind our *siddurim,*
prayer books, taking turns sounding
out the words, one syllable at a time.

To get to that basement classroom
in Temple Ahavath Achim — Love
of Brothers (why not Sisters, too?) —
I walked down my block: East Second

to Avenue P, past Katz's Appetizer,
where every week Mom sent me
to buy chub white fish, smoked
in their gold scaly skins or Nova lox.

For hours I could've watched Mr. Katz
sharpen his two steel knives, squealing
blade against blade, then slice smoked
salmon thin as strudel dough. A quarter

pound for four. Bagels I bought at Streit's
next door, onion my favorite, smothered
top to bottom in shiny slivers. Intoxicated
by the smell, I'd chew my way

to Jerry's Market. In summer, a green awning
like a beach umbrella protected peaches
and plums. In winter, sawdust on wood
floors kept customers from slipping on slush.

Below Jerry's cash register, rows of apples
and pears. Once I saw a twenty perched on
a red delicious like a butterfly and gave
it to Jerry. "You're an honest girl." But

when I got home, instead of praising, Mom's
blue eyes turned black. "Twenty dollars! So
much money! Jerry put it in his pocket."
I didn't know whether to shrink or grow.

   * * *

Years later, *shalom* became good-bye
to my favorite uncle. At fifty-six, Uncle
Abie died. A cutter, the fur blackened
his lungs. "As if he'd smoked three packs

a day," his doctor said. Blue eyes and smiling
mouth, Uncle Abie paid me a nickel
each time I pulled Uncle Yorgie's tie.
Mom said when I was a baby, on Sundays

Uncle Abie walked me miles in my hand-me-
down carriage. "Once his hands slipped,

the carriage almost ran away." At the cemetery,
Aunt Lilly tried to jump into his grave, but

Cousin Howie held her tight against his chest.
In my only black jacket and skirt and not
wearing lipstick, I said "Shalom, Uncle Abie."
My father passed at eighty. For two years

after his heart attack, triple by-pass,
kidney failure, Mom couldn't say *shalom*.
"No matter what, it's better here
than in the dirt."

ZURAWNO LADIES' AUXILIARY

I remember Mom at the full-length mirror checking
if her slip peeked out of her chic black and white
dress, quickly lip-sticking, powdering and lightly

rouging her cheeks. I remember those 3-cent
postcards from Mollie Armel, Secretary, her Old World
Polish cursive, her letters flowing like the Dniester;

and Mom, once a month, going by subway to the Lower East Side
to lunch with the ladies at Ratner's. And I wondered
if I skipped school, could I ever learn the real history

by sitting with those ladies at the table, eating
butter-fried pirogen slathered in sour cream?

DREAM: THE HANGING

Judy, my camp counselor,
opens the gate.
I stand where the bunks
used to be.

      The apple tree
branches are spindly, the trunk
too thin. Everything is crooked.

No children.
No dinner bell.

Two men
drag a body. A long black cloak
      and hood.

"Thief! She stole potato peels."

"Hang her!" Judy orders.

      *   *   *

Brooklyn, our kitchen.
Even the dream radio reports

Julius and Ethel Rosenberg
died in the Electric Chair.

I twirl my pigtail. Mom

sits at the table, crying.

She asks how
in America
a Jewish judge and jury

could have convicted them.
Why the President
refused?

      *   *   *

The woman stands alone.

"Stop!" I scream to Judy, but
her uncle hammers his gavel.

A wild wind blows
through the crowd.

Judy's men push away
the stool.

The woman's heart
beats weaker, weaker.
Her still-warm blood
meets mine.

DIALOGUE

Stop bleeding   said the mother-to-be
I would if I could   said the uterus
I'm breathing slow and deep   can't
you just relax   said the mother-to-be
No way I'm   not in charge just follow
orders from higher   up to push clots out
Who runs this bloody show
Damned if know   said the uterus   aren't
you the one who went to school
Yes said the mother-to-be   that's why I'm
keeping as still as I can   in this hospital bed
what else would help   you stop bleeding
Too late   to shut the gate said the uterus
no other way   to go but out
Stop   shouted the mother-to-be   for so many
years I put up   with your bloody periods   prayed
for the day   finally I'd conceive
I know it's been   rough said the uterus
Stop bleeding   pleaded the mother-to-be
for fourteen weeks I've loved   this
baby   please don't take her   away
How many times   do I have to say
it's not my call   I can't do anything
to keep her   safe said the uterus
Cry with me   said the mother-to-be

FIRST MS ATTACK

i was entering my twenty-fourth year
when a bolt of lightning
struck my knee & sparks flew toe to thigh

six weeks married   i had no time
for anything but sex & teaching
still   fears sneaked in

through the door that didn't shut
till I gave myself to doctors
believing they knew   everything

or with a snap of fingers
their genie   would figure it out
did you & your husband fight

asked the hospital physician   this
could be   newly-married hysteria
(Freud twisting weeping women's

minds around icy bodies) no
i said   from my bed i watched
leaves on the maple tree outside

shrivel & flee across the street
in between   as perfect patient i
was passed from machine to machine

REGRETS

I stare out the window of my pine-paneled study.
Half the hemlock waves in wind, the rest hides
behind the side of the house. What others see —
smiles or frowns, dress-up or dress-down clothes —
conceal or reveal what I choose to show.
I shudder to remember how I hid the truth

of my illness from Mom and Dad, afraid truth
would hurt them. Holocaust survivors. An A+ student
through my Ph.D., I believed I had to be perfect, not show
I had MS, a disease their sixty-ish neighbor couldn't hide.
Despite her life bound to a wheelchair, she was clothed
in love from her husband and mother. Mom and Dad saw,

admired their devotion. But Mom's words chain-sawed
through: "What a terrible old age for her mother!" True.
As my legs grew weaker, how could I disclose?
"I'm too busy to walk with you," I lied, staying in my study.
"Your legs will forget how," Mom said, not hiding
her annoyance. But how could I let my jello-legs show?

A mistake I can't take back, too late to show
how, in my late forties, I tried to protect them from seeing
my leg-muscles tighten, refuse to make another step, by hiding
in front of my desktop computer screen to block truth
or by pulling pachysandra from the walk outside my study
on hands and knees, sweating in summer clothes.

Dad passed at eighty, two years later. I tore my clothes,
sat *Shiva* with Mom, letting our love show.
From our hearts we talked, sitting on the sofa in my study.

"We thought you didn't love us. We didn't see
you couldn't walk." I pulled Mom close. "Not true!
I didn't want you to see and suffer, so I hid."

"Come live with me in Delray Beach. Stop hiding.
I'll care for you, bring this nightmare to a close."
  If only this could come true.
  But I know MS is showier:
Secondary Progressive, my neurologists saw.
Not even Mom's love could undo medical studies.

A lifetime can't hide mistakes that don't show.
This truth pursues me like a door that won't close.
Alone in my pine-paneled study, this is what I see.

MULTIPLE SCLEROSIS

I

We live in bodies clumsy and disobedient,
wake to urine-soaked pajama pants, or a warning
twinge before bowels unravel, foul the bed;
wake to waves of chill-chattering teeth, fever
firing seizures, hallucinations of the dead
dancing in air above our heads.

II

Leg spasms
split night,
my right
toes twist
into tortured
poses, my
hamstrings
kick, kicking
my legs
in time
to an ecstatic
drummer
beating
his *djembe*
dizzy.

III

Yesterday
at the gym

in the locker room
when the stainless
steel transfer bar
behind the slatted
shower bench
snapped
off the tiled wall
with me
a paraplegic
dangling mid-air
between bench
and wheelchair,
you
my guardian angel
cradled me.

IV

It is good
to skim even a stiff body
through a school
of swimmers, catching
their kicks, free-floating
atoms of energy, back
and forth for an hour,
forgetting the invisible
hand, all night
squeezing an ankle
till sleep disappears
in tears and screams.

It is good
to loiter in the locker room
to watch morning
parade past in Speedo
or skirted suits, a one-
breasted woman
scratch her sprouting
scalp, an anorexic
with legs like toothpicks
skip the required shower, a senior
hunch her way to a bench.

It is good
to punch the automatic
door opener and crunch
through late November's
wind-blown leaves, to breathe
in cold clear air, a preview
of snow, to press one button
on a black remote and watch
my mini-van door
slide open, the ramp unfold,
to ride up, look forward, lock down.

LIKE SISTERS, AN ELEGY

I

There was the day we swam
across the Vermont pond, late
May chilly water clawing
our feet. You stroked and kicked
like an Olympian while I
dog-paddled in your wake,
legs scissored shut as I struggled
not to sink. On my back, I floated
to safety, where you lay sprawled
on grassy weeds like a turtle sunning.
"What took you?" you asked, one hand
shading your deep brown eyes.
"Icy water," I answered, instead of
I almost drowned.

II

Genie from Queens, Joanie from Flatbush.
"My parents couldn't spell," you laughed,
when we met as MFA roommates.
With your sprained ankle and my off-balance
hesitation, arm-in-arm we crisscrossed
the college quad. "Are you two sisters?"
classmates asked. Sitting on my bed
or yours, late evenings we shared secrets.
One of your lovers, the famous
landscape artist (married, of course)
stroked your body as if it were his

most vibrant canvas. My fear:
one day I'd wake
in a fouled bed,
my scarred nerve cells short-circuited
like a frayed electric wire, my body
a headstone unable to budge.

III

The end of our twelve-day
residency, I watched you
fold your sweatshirt, zip
your suitcase closed. "See you
at home, Sister," I said. "No,"
you answered, "we're residency friends."

IV

Six months later, you burst
into our room, plopped your suitcase
on your bed, squeezed your arms
around me. "Look," you said, holding
out your left hand, on your ring finger
a gold band. "Bill's a great guy!
It took me three times
to get this right," you laughed.

V

Twenty-four years gone by, seasons
as unpredictable as the river

outside my studio window. Once
in awhile, at weekend writing retreats,
we bumped into each other: two women
unafraid of going gray. You never told me
of your first cancer scare. This morning,
I study the photo someone snapped
at our last session, you sitting on the rug
beside me, I in my electric wheelchair,
our hands clasping each others' tight,
not ready to let go of this residency on earth.

TRAILS

I've always wanted to tell you,
Maggie, how patiently snow sits
on the hill outside my window

waiting for thirsty deer to track
their path to the tree-lined stream.
Do you remember daybreak,

our hike on the mesa trail
when walking was as easy for me
as riding a horse was for you?

Silently
a doe and her fawn
stepped out of the mist

like apparitions. We
watched them stare back, afraid
one move would shoot them past

the aspens. How long before they
turned, vanished into the mist,
leaving us at once bereft and blessed?

LATKES

Each week by heart
I punch your land-line.
Half the time it's David

answering your phone. "Joan's
napping on the couch." The old
days, that's where we sat,

sipping tea while you
critiqued another new poem
I rushed to show. Last month

you called from the hospital.
Another transfusion. Your old
voice, sassy and strong. "Now

I know why vampires like blood."
This first day of Hanukkah,
my kitchen smells of latkes

sizzling in peanut oil. For you
in foil I pack a batch, drive
quick before they cool.

RIBBONS

I

Your voice on my answering machine:
"It's been a rough road but I'm back."
Back from another taxi ride
to the Emergency Room.
Back from another hospital stay.
Back from vomiting black bile,
your body's guts rebelling
against a lifetime of common sense.
"Had I known I would have eaten
all those McDonald's fries,
all those KFC chicken pot pies,
all those Domino's pepperoni pizzas."

II

Closest cousin from my childhood,
your long blonde page-boy frames a face
that could grace the cover of *Seventeen*.
In pigtails and Mary Janes, after snack
I skip across the hall to your apartment.
For a few minutes, I sit on your bed, dizzy
from the Jean Naté you sprayed on yourself
before leaving for high school. Some days
I study sketches of sexy dresses you designed
or explore your top drawer until that afternoon
you caught me with your pink and purple
ribbons rolled around my fingers. "Sorry."

I still taste the cake of Lifebuoy soap
you shoved into my mouth, your hands clamping
my jaw shut, jamming my teeth deep into the bar.

III

Salt water and sand in your hair, you
meet your future husband on the Boardwalk
at Brighton Beach. A photography student,
shirt smelling like darkroom chemicals,
he makes you laugh, snapping non-stop, insisting
one of his black-and-whites will win,
will make you Miss Subways, your face
smiling on posters in every New York train.

IV

To support you and his empty portrait studio,
most nights your husband delivers the *Jewish
Daily Forward,* comes home with fingers
black from newsprint. Instead of letting you
find a job, he insists you sit by the bed, waiting
for him to wake late morning to have sex.
If not, his screams and slaps shake the walls.
For years you choose to comply, so your girls
won't hear or see, so no one knows.

V

At the kitchen table, you skim the Want Ads
of the New York Post, check *Receptionist, Dentist's
office, Sales clerk, Macy's.* Your determination
shuts out the squeaks, his footsteps down the stairs.
He grabs the paper, swats your coffee.
You move away from his rage, his sweat.
He yanks you by the hair, pulls you up
the stairs. Your teenage daughter,
cramming for finals, bangs open her door.
He lets go. "See what you made me do!"

VI

Like sparrows your words fly: from your mother
to mine to me. Years after your divorce,
our mothers still blame you. As if living
in Zurawno, not Flatbush, they repeat:
"It's a wife's duty to please her husband."
At the kitchen table, they sip Sanka,
shake their heads when I point to the *Post:*
"Husband beats wife to death."
"Not Ruth's husband, he loved her." The hair
on my arms stands straight.

VII

Rush hour, you stand holding tight
to the subway pole, swaying to the jerky
stops and starts, closing your nose to morning
shampoo smells, evening sour sweat. One night

coming back from your bookkeeping job,
squeezed in a seat, drifting in and out of sleep,
you open your eyes to see him standing
over you, his right hand balancing his body
on the shifting trapeze overhead. "Ruchel," he whispers,
your Yiddish name. You close your eyes.
When you open them, he is gone.

VIII

Back and forth you fly, almost a commuter
to Lod Airport. Your widowed mother at seventy,
escaped her new husband by *making Aliyah* — ("He
forced her to do disgusting things like suck
his dingle," my mother says) — but by ninety,
she needs you to tell her what to eat and what to wear,
as if you live in the old walk-up, as if you are her mother.

IX

A rainy night on Broadway, inside the empty
theater, the usher ignores your mezzanine seat,
puts you in the orchestra beside a man with wisps
of white hair. At intermission, your smile and comments
on the play are as useless as a microphone
to coax conversation. As you turn to leave, he taps
your shoulder, waves two tickets to next week's
Mozart. Like a boy asking for a first date, he stutters
an invitation. Over months of concerts, plays, dinners,
he shows you photos of his deceased wife
of forty-six years, takes you to meet their three sons,
grandchildren. You become his best friend and lover,

and teach him intimacy, how for the first time
to give himself to another.

X

In the early morning haze of dreams,
you visit me today, a first in the three years
since you died. Your face radiant, your skin
fragrant as rose water, your voice
an unstoppable fountain. "Look, my newest line,
Joanie nightgowns. Want to try
one on?" Your fingers slip the silk
over my head, help thread my arms
through the lace-trimmed straps, adjust
the fabric around my breasts, tie
the pink and purple ribbons in a bow.

THE COUGH

wracked her ribs. All summer
my daughter spat, steamed

in a toweled tent. At a friend's
violin recital, a stranger hushed her,

his shush a slap.
As if she could keep her cough

prisoner, chained deep inside her chest,
simply by sealing her lips.

When September arrived,
my daughter found her own apartment,

a new job. At her kitchen table,
she sat sucking black Chinese pellets

up a straw, letting them melt
on her tongue. *Asthma.*

Winter deepened her cough.
She developed an itch so insistent

at night she became the cat
who scratched her legs bloody.

In daylight through her stockings
streaks of scars I never noticed. "Why?"

one of her colleagues asked. Like a caught
criminal, she kept quiet. At night if she slipped

into a shallow sleep, she woke soaked
in sweat, details she told only her naturopath.

At the end of the summer,
a physician friend noticed a lump

along her throat. Like a golf ball,
the oncologist said. And yet

the naturopath never noticed.
And worse, nor did I.

In my nightmares I hear Jen cough, see
her thin, drawn face begin to disappear.

RESCUE

My mother, Frances Reiss, *zichrono li shalom*,
passed away four weeks short of ninety:
lymphoma beat dementia by a hair.
Twenty years she lived in a villa in Delray Beach.

Mom passed away four weeks short of ninety.
Before, her neighbors warned, "Don't let her live alone."
For twenty years Mom loved her villa in Delray Beach.
Frightened, I hired an aide four hours a day to keep an eye

after her neighbors warned, "Don't let her live alone."
Mom fired every aide I hired – "She steals."
I hired an aide four hours a day to keep an eye.
"She sits and watches me cook and clean."

Mom fired every aide I hired – "She steals."
Spring Break, I came to see what's what.
"She sits and watches me cook and clean."
At 2 a.m. Mom barreled past my bed.

Spring Break, I came to see what's what.
In her nightgown, Mom headed for the door.
At 2 a.m. she barreled past my bed.
"Where are you going?" I grabbed her hand.

In her nightgown, Mom opened the door.
"I hear Sol calling. He drives me to my doctors."
I grabbed her hand and led her back to bed.
I saved Mom from falling down her stone steps.

"I hear Sol calling. He drives me to my doctors."
A miracle, I was there to prevent catastrophe.
I saved Mom from falling down her stone steps.
I saved Mom from another fractured hip or worse.

A miracle, I was there to prevent catastrophe.
"Mom, I'm taking you home with me."
I saved her from another fractured hip or worse.
"Okay. I don't know why, but lately I feel funny."

Mom, you're coming home with me."
I baked her honey cake and made a farewell party.
"Okay. I don't know why, but lately I feel funny."
She lay on my couch; the fever kept coming back.

I baked her honey cake and made a farewell party.
For tests, my doctor put Mom in the hospital
after she lay on my couch and her fever kept coming back.
Nurses diapered her, sat her in a wheelchair.

For tests, my doctor put Mom in the hospital.
I needed to feed her, she couldn't hold a spoon.
Nurses diapered her, sat her in a wheelchair.
I moved Mom to a nursing home, five minutes away.

I needed to feed her, she couldn't hold a spoon.
I moved Mom to a nursing home five minutes away.
Lymphoma beat dementia by a hair.
My mother, Frances Reiss, *zichrono li shalom*.

VOICES

I watched the ultrasound screen:
on the right half of my thyroid
a Cyclops in black and white.

"That mass in the middle's a node.
Fifty percent of people
have one, even me," my doctor said.

Next, a fine needle biopsy, five tries
to pierce the calcified rim, like breaking
through an eggshell. Results: "Inconclusive,

a follicular neoplasm," my doctor said.
What does that mean? I wanted to scream.
Malignant or benign? To know

requires removing my right thyroid.
Each day I pray for guidance.
From deep inside of me, stutter-free,

Don't! the voice says. *Do!* my doctor says.

Four and a half weeks after surgery:
"Minimally invasive follicular neoplasm
carcinoma," my doctor says.

But my inner voice? God's voice? Or
my voice inventing what I want to hear
like dialogue in a story I write?

God give us back the days
when You spoke
to us all, even slaves.
When You promised Hagar
she would become
mother of a mighty nation.
When you told Moses
to lead the Israelites out of Egypt.

Free me from my cacophony, let me
hear You speak.

FIRST VISIT TO MAGGIE'S RANCH

Summer sun bakes sagebrush, rattlesnakes
haunt the heat. Fearless, each day you stroll
your rolling hills of tumbleweed and dust, your prairie

paradise. "More miles than Manhattan," you say.
You need twenty acres to water one cow.
We jeep around your boundaries

checking for cracked fences, unlatched gates,
stop at a windmill, watch water
fill a wooden trough. Further along at another

edge of your land a stand of weeping willows
where a creek from the South Platte trickles.
The perfect place to sit on stumps, chew

juicy papaya with dark, dark chocolate.
Late afternoon back at the corral you
whistle for your sleek black horse, saddle up.

Your ranch-hand steps out of the stable, lifts
me like a child to sit behind you. I look down
wishing the ground were nearer, wishing

all those years of watching "Bonanza"
could make me feel at ease. But, clippity-clop
as Thunder gallops I squeeze tightly.

"Relax! you're squishing my breasts," you say,
laughing. "Sorry, it's my first time." Your left
hand brushes mine, your right pulls lightly

back on the reins to slow the pace. We head
into the sunset singing "Don't Fence Me In."

HILLS AND VALLEYS

I never wanted to know
what it was like
to reach for a word —
take "knee," for example,
my left a favorite
for folding to my chest
when MS spasms send me reeling —
and find instead a silent stutter.

In the hospital after her stroke
your mother, pointing
to her knees, croaked,
"Cover these hills."

Twenty-three years later
your third recurrence, chemo
weekly to soothe the pain.
Too many hours
on the sofa. Today
I won't stay long.

Before I learned
to drive again — instead of my right
foot, my left hand pressing the knob
for gas and brake — you'd take me
to the A&P, unfold then fold
my first wheelchair, pivot me
out then back into your Saab.

A few times a week
we speak — as if we'll be here

forever — about New England winters
the snowstorms, shoveling our driveways
side by side, and about our sons,
their children now old enough,
for airplane visits alone.

Passover seders
at my table or yours,
four times refilling goblets
with blackberry wine. Brisket,
leg of lamb, tzimmes,
kugel overflowing our plates.
You or I motioning
to the open door, urging
Elijah to step right in.

SHARONI, REMEMBER

Sharoni, remember how much
you were loved, the hands
that caressed your breasts, the lips
that kissed the iris of your sex.

Sharoni, remember those Oakland
women shivering in the street,
their bodies blue-black welts of fear
until you led them safely to shelter.

Sharoni, remember the Chilean village,
its name an anonymous whisper, where you
taught young women already as old
as their mothers secrets they needed to know.

Sharoni, remember why you studied
social work: to care for your parents
when time would trip their steps
or take away their words.

Sharoni, I remember, young cousin,
when you swept away your curls, showed me
the map of three surgeries which couldn't keep
your tumor from creeping like bittersweet.

FOR MY FRIEND FIGHTING BREAST CANCER

I wanted to show you where I spotted
the cardinals building their nest. Rare
to see such a couple making themselves
at home in my backyard. Look, high up there

in the crotch of that leafy branch, almost
concealed by the neighboring Japanese
maple. Like our teenage sons they
stay busy, flying back and forth too many

times to count. But these birds know
their purpose, rush to scavenge and weave
bits of scrap and twigs. In no time,
we'll see red threads peek through

their finished nest, the female sitting still,
incubating her eggs. In no time, the chicks
will crack through. In no time, the female
will push her fledglings to fly. In no time,

we'll look up to see only red threads
peeking through this weave of leaves.
I know, dear one, you worry
for your son. Unlike these cardinals,

how long a lifetime do we mothers need?

KATHY SHAUGHNESSY JAMBECK

(1956-2012)

Your dying left an empty seat across
my dining room table. Starlight still shines
through the bay window.
Your name blazes its trail of memories and loss:
how you feared for your son,
the star in your constellation, too young
to watch you flicker, fade, disappear.

FOR BETTER OR WORSE

Oh poems, if only you would come
with words like a wizard whisking me
to a place I've longed to see
but never knew existed. At daybreak if I sit
in my pine-paneled study by the window
watching sparrows flit branch to branch,
could I count on your appearance as I do
on my husband, who reaches for my hands
to help me out of bed; who dances me
from chair to toilet to shower; who
slides the towel between each toe to dry;
who straightens my shirt, pulls up my pants,
puts on my socks and shoes?
                          Oh poems, do I ask
too much of you who have not been at my side
for forty-five years? Oh husband, do I ask
too much of you?

THERE'S NO APP FOR THAT

This is the hand
that led you to bed.

This is the hand
that caressed your head.

This is the hand
that unbuckled your belt.

This is the hand
that unzipped your pants.

This is the hand
that stroked your sex.

This is the hand
that slid you in deep,

that rocked your buttocks,
that squeezed you past sleep.

POSSIBILITIES

I prefer 3-speed bikes, the black Schwinn I pedaled cross-country.
I prefer roller skates that clatter on pavement.
I prefer granddaughters to the grandsons I don't have.
I prefer telling the truth
though the truth doesn't always need to be told.
J'adore parler français et vivre en France.
I prefer one long marriage
to several short affairs.
I would prefer to swim the Australian crawl
than be tingled by a French tickler.
I prefer not to live with clutter
though clutter prefers to live with me.
I prefer deadlines.
I'd prefer to die before my spouse, to give him time
to find another sexy wife, but one
who could put her clothes back on without help.
I prefer weeping willows along the Dniester.
I prefer to forgive but not always to forget.
I would prefer to schuss straight down the ski slope
in my bi-ski than crisscross the mountain side to side.
I prefer non-stop flights and flight attendants
strong enough to carry me to the toilet.
I prefer to believe in possibilities,
that my brain is creating new pathways
to let me walk again.

IN MY DREAM

I am standing in a field of just-cut hay, the yellow straw
smell embracing me like a lost love. Gone are my wheel-
chair years, gone the rolling walker that came before, gone
my bamboo ski poles transformed to canes. If only Mom,
whose body last I knew these past eleven years was resting
next to Dad's in the New Jersey cemetery I never visit,
convinced as I am their spirits have long since abandoned
the dark mahogany coffins Mom insisted on ordering
to keep the worms away from their flesh longer than pine boxes —
if only she were here to see, after all those years paying for
uninsured alternative treatments while wishing, wishing, wishing
this illness would disappear and let me walk again.
As if this were not miracle enough, I look up to see Mom
come flying down the hill, holding tight to the handles
of her great-granddaughter Tali's jogging stroller,
smiling all the while those two take the ride of their lives.

LE CHEMIN DE GUÉRISON INTÉRIEURE: ROAD OF INNER HEALING

I

Through morning mist, a church spire rises,
surrounded by hectares of hay fields.
Late summer baled cylinders of straw.

ST. ANTOINE L'ABBAYE.

But I haven't come as a tourist
to visit this Medieval crypt or to bow down and pray.

I have long been a Jew turned from God.

Ski poles for balance, I climb stone stairs,
struggle to open the oak door at l'Arche.
All along the stone corridor, my footsteps echo. I turn to run,

as if my feet haven't forgotten how,
as if already they've been healed.

II

Twice a day, lectures on how to heal *spiritual, physical, psychic wounds to become whole, giving life back to the depths of being.* I sit, scribbling notes in French, as if a schoolgirl taking *Dictation:*

*God is not a being detached from man to be sought after
but a power that seeks, pursues, calls upon man.*

It's God who knocks and waits for us to open the door.
Offer your difficulty to God, like Joshua with the walls of Jericho.

The words pique like bees. Where was God when my grandparents
called Him, before their Ukrainian neighbors shot
then tossed their still breathing bodies in a pit of Zurawno's Jews?

Where is He now, amidst this world aflame?

Abandon the desire to understand; accept your reality, your human limits.

III

Outside bells toll, an hourly reminder.

We are here to bear witness and experience the Divine in daily life,
a road with no other destination.

> Running, walking, sitting, talking, singing in a circle,
> hand in hand, folk-dancing in the garden,
> blackberry brambles, beetles, butterflies,
> whatever my body permits, I do.

In the end, I pray:

My heart is ready, O God, my heart is ready.

NOTES

Page 4: "Why My Mother Can't Speak Yiddish." *Du host genug gekvetsht!* (Yiddish): "You have complained enough already." *Rozinkes mit Mandlen* (Carrots with Almonds) was a popular Yiddish lullaby.

Page 10: "Hiding from the Nazis" is for Sam Jonas.

Page 12: "A Bielski Partisan Speaks." *Otriad* is Russian for a partisan unit; *shtetl* (Yiddish) refers to the tightly knit Jewish community way of life that existed throughout Eastern Europe before the Holocaust. This poem is for Nechama Tec.

Page 15: "My Mother Writes a Letter Home." HIAS is an acronym for the Hebrew Immigration Aid Society.

Page 17: "Rue Ordener, Rue Labat" is for Michèle Ganem.

Page 19: "Cousin" is for Nechama Tec.

Page 20: "My Cousin Tells How His Brother Found Him" is for Stan Ostern.

Page 24: "On Approaching Seventy" is for Ray.

Page 36: "Regrets." *Shiva:* Yiddish for the traditional seven days of mourning.

Page 38: "Multiple Sclerosis." *We live in bodies clumsy and disobedient* is from Ellen Doré Watson's poem, "We Live in Bodies."

Page 41: Like Sisters, an Elegy" is for the late Genie Zeiger.

Page 44: "Trails" is for Maggie Atkinson.

Page 45: "Latkes" is for the late Joan Joffe Hall.

Page 46: "Ribbons" is for my late Cousin Ruth.

Page 51: "The Cough" is for Jen.

Page 53: "Rescue." The phrase *zichrono li shalom* (Hebrew) literally means "her memory to peace."

Page 57: "First Visit to Maggie's Ranch" is for Maggie Atkinson.

Page 58: "Hills and Valleys" is for the late Joan Joffe Hall.

Page 60: "Sharoni, Remember" is for Nurit Mussen, the late Sharoni's mother.

Page 65: "Possibilities." *J'adore parler français et vivre en France*: "I adore speaking French and living in France."

Page 67: "Le Chemin de Guérison Intérieure: Road of Inner Healing." The poem refers to a year-long workshop series designed by Simone Pacot, offered at l'Arche in St. Antoine l'Abbaye, a non-violent ecumenical Christian community, one of several founded by Lanza del Vasto after his encounter with Gandhi.

ABOUT THE AUTHOR

Joan Seliger Sidney grew up with parents who barely escaped the Holocaust, unlike her grandparents and other relatives who did not. The story of those forebears along with the desire to learn more about Jewish life in her family's hometown of Zurawno, Poland, led Joan to the Fortunoff Video Archives for Holocaust Testimonies on a Visiting Faculty Fellowship from Yale, to continue writing poems, both imagined and true, bearing witness to the Holocaust. How to make peace and live well with secondary-progressive Multiple Sclerosis has been another recurrent and sometimes interwoven theme. Her books include *Body of Diminishing Motion: Poems and a Memoir* (CavanKerry Press) and *The Way the Past Comes Back* (The Kutenai Press). Her poems have appeared in *The Louisville Review, The Massachusetts Review, Michigan Quarterly Review, Jewish Currents, Caduceus, Theodate,* and elsewhere. They have also been anthologized in *Beyond Lament, Her Face in the Mirror, Points of Contact, Touching MS, Moments in Time, Range of Motion,* and *Anthology of Magazine Verse & Yearbook of American Poetry.* Joan has received individual artist's poetry fellowships from the Connecticut Commission on the Arts, the Connecticut Commission on Culture and Tourism, the Craig H. Neilsen Foundation, the Christopher Reeve Paralysis Foundation, and Vermont Studio Center. She lived and sometimes taught near Grenoble, France, and has also taught at the University of Connecticut and Eastern Connecticut State University. She is currently writer-in-residence at the University of Connecticut's Center for Judaic Studies and Contemporary Jewish Life. In addition, Joan facilitates "Writing for Your Life," an adult workshop. She lives with her husband of forty-eight years in Storrs, Connecticut. They are the parents of four children and five granddaughters.

This book has been set in Perpetua, designer Eric Gill's most celebrated
typeface. The clean, chiseled look of this font reflects
its creator's stonecutting work.

To order additional copies of this book
or other Antrim House titles, contact the publisher at

Antrim House
21 Goodrich Rd., Simsbury, CT 06070
860.217.0023, AntrimHouse@comcast.net
or the house website (www.AntrimHouseBooks.com).

•

On the house website
in addition to information on books
you will find sample poems, upcoming events,
and a "seminar room" featuring supplemental biography,
notes, images, poems, reviews, and
writing suggestions.